Poems of This Century
and
Poems of the Last Century

This volume includes the second edition of *Strange Intimate Union* now called *Poems of The Last Century*.
First published in India in 1986

Poems of This Century and Poems of the Last Century

www.imosfoundation.org

Published by The Conrad Press in the United Kingdom 2024

Tel: +44(0)1227 472 874
www.theconradpress.com
info@theconradpress.com

ISBN 978-1-916966-72-7

Typesetting and Cover Design by: Charlotte Mouncey, www.bookstyle.co.uk

Printed and bound in Great Britain by Clays Ltd, Elcograf S.p.A.

To honour those who have given me the ability
to realise dreams and offered the love that
changes life for the better.

Poems of This Century

and

Poems of the Last Century

Briony Kapoor

Introduction

I began writing poetry at the age of thirty-three after an epiphany. I was alone in the Himalayas at the time. It was piercingly the most relevant experience of my life. The epiphany, I mean, and the poetry flowed afterwards.

At the time I assumed the epiphany was from God. After a few weeks of extraordinary bliss however, I wanted to be grounded again, though with my new and special knowledge. I wanted to be a witness in the world for this thing, I took, at the time, to be God.

It is certainly the closest thing to God. I called my first volume of poetry Strange Intimate Union because of it. I believed it to be a direct experience of the divine. I still do but that the sobering years have made me realise it is only itself, not a proof of any kind.

The experience changed me for the better. It confirmed in me a confidence in life, in love, in the possibility of goodness. It gave me renewed access to joy and I have always moved forward thereafter on a highway of happiness.

The first volume *Strange Intimate Union* seems to me to brimming with love to an almost overwhelming degree. A result perhaps of my love for my husband and the impact of my new experience. This second one is quite different with poems falling into numerous categories. For every poem I write down there is another that came to me that I did not write down.

If I were to read these two slim volumes I would want to experience what the writer attempts to express. Because I actually am the writer, I did experience it all. I am so very grateful to have danced in the creation as I am still most fortunately able to do.

Briony Kapoor November 2024

Poems of this Century
Post Millenium, Older Woman

Introduction

After a gap of about twenty years I began writing poetry again in my early fifties. By this time I had been long back in England living with my elderly mother whom I looked after for many years. I had made my fortune with hard work but I had become a widow in tragic circumstances.

These later poems also fall into several groups. Many of the themes are similar. I remain much concerned with the love of man and with the idea of God, with nature and with philosophical speculation. There are differences though from the writing of my younger self.

I am now an individual living an independent life on my own terms. As happens to all humans as they advance in time, I am marked by the pain of various life events. Still full of love and hope and supported by that early epiphany, I am nevertheless more thoughtful and more compassionate towards the human condition as it affects others as well as myself.

I have learned the value of friends and become sensible to the importance of the communication by identity of women. Indeed I believe women are a greater source of strength to me than men. Despite my enjoyment of them, I take men less seriously than I did in the romantic dreams of my younger self.

I care for the noble ideals of the European Union and support the highest ideals of politics. I admire the great works of human civilisations and am deeply moved by the achievements of the best and greatest individuals amongst them.

I see and appreciate the modest goodness of everyday people of many backgrounds and have faith in common decency and kindness. I celebrate quiet significant talent. I am glad to be a part of this side of humanity. Although I have significant doubts about it, I have hope for the outcome for ourselves and the greater forces of creation.

I have divided these sixty-six poems into seven sections or chaps by subject.

Briony Kapoor November 2024

Contents of the First Volume Section One

Thoughtful, Religious and Philosophical Poems

1. God Poem   (08.01.19)

I belong to a God in whom I don't believe
How does this curious contradiction live?
A strange idea that cannot be
But that at least is truth and truth for me

It seems mere words make little sense
Illuminating the immense
In huge dimensions now the mind
A wordless something looks to find

This certain and more certain thing ...
Does overwhelming satisfaction bring
A deep identity confirmed
A meaning ultimately earned

Truths of vast importance are ...
Maybe within or may come from afar
What is inside or what without
When reason finds itself in doubt?

Exists or not, we ponder, it's obscure
A baffled language won't admit to cure
The Godlike thing it is ... does cheerfully persist
And whatever, being or non being, will insist

2. Involuntary

Involunt'ry we're gifted life
And come to be alive
This disconcerting present is
A puzzling surprise

Our eyes are opened on the world
All senses brought to life
Before we have the judgement to
Assess the baffling prize

Flash in a dark eternal
We open like God's eye
To a splendour of creation
We scale by our own time

Perhaps with eagerness, with love,
We feast at all the board
But many random humans know
Much less of life's reward

If birthed unwilling to a hand
What can human do?
Grapple a bit to try and fit
Or play it true and through

Given we suffer with the pain
Bestowed exotic potion
Direct our interest to the best
Desire and fine emotion

Is there a path that makes it good
Different for every One?
Unknowing, we must make a way
Involunt'ry begun

3. Cogent

There are two higher powers
Goodness and the creative force
Goodness pertains to humans
Also perhaps their chosen creatures
The planet, by God, is something else
So blue, so tiny - seen from elsewhere
So huge, so green, so generous to us here

An element, a life, the great
Variety of things
And one becomes another
Deeper ... complex ...organic ...
By way of time.
Time the catalyst stolen from eternity
To ends diverse. It grows, egglike
To hatch to what? We do not know.

Spread through a billion years
And each eye a glimpse of glory
No matter the pain but
How it hurt in a single life
And then when it didn't, inert
What a choice
(But that, too, a brief illusion).

Me, I laugh with the wind
Take joy in flowering and
Watch the sky for wild clouds
Out in the world
Blent in a fragile weave
Soon, too soon and leave.
Where I? Where it?

And goodness unwilled
Inevitable in acceptance
It is a kind of worship
I'm confined in the manner
Stretched to the possible
And God nowhere to be seen
In this declaration of happiness
Only permeating reality with the
Goodness we feel and be and do.

4. Clamour

There's been clamour
And I do not like it
Coming like reality
In knots and nonsense
Or swirled like muck in water
Where clarity could be

Like the muddle keys
On the top line of a typewriter
£&@"?!(&£/:;@&&"?!
Through a glass darkly
But you carried on clumsy
And a little sad

Against a day of renewal
You had not an inkling
Just a general sinking
Or a stumble in the aisle
That rises up there

5. Sonnet

Will all our joys come to a dismal end
Should now our lives be blighted and descend
If middle aged we are or are to be
Or might we find it satisfactory?
Those subtle pleasures, humble minor loves
For which to date we've never cared enough
Like choosing right much more than we choose wrong
Emerge now quietly and they seem quite strong.
An aspirating quality, an aire
A humming space inside where we belong
A thing that we can have and also share
Like owning the deep throbbing part of song
Ignore the softened edges blunted hope
A cornucopia is infinite in scope

6. Towards

I move towards the realm of God
(A God I don't believe in)
A place that's here, a time that's now
I'm at it or within

So many ways of having this
Just lying here alone
I'm not the only one I know
To whom these states are known

A kind of Being in oneself
Obtaining to the show
Becomes a person all throughout
A soaring rise or flow

In wholly strength, with world-blind eye
We are towards and bring
To life itself that coming forth
When one is Everything

To speak of joy is not enough
Though joy is in the state
Its continuity reveals
The way that things relate

Unknowing Cloud and Fire of Love
Or Lightness of the Being
All Will Be Well ... we hear the words
Tell clarity of Seeing

7. Free Will Poem

I am an individual
There are some things I do
I thought I had my own Free Will
But now I'm told that it's not true

My person (who's not me at all)
A thing all of it's own
Collects up my experience
And sets our path alone

Those selfish genes will do their thing
And I am not to blame
(It is a wonder if I'm good
When being bad is just the same)

We have our inclinations
And will do what we do
Though tempered by our memories
To basic body selves we're true

It's just as if we're walking twins
The larger part decides
But kindly lets us think with us
Responsibility resides

Our genial lusts and greedy ways
Are how we really spend our days
While wise directions and just acts
Are not a credit but just facts

The thinking person that is ME
Is just a construct and a tool
What is the point of it, to be
A grand illusion and a fool?

So given that I am not here
God wouldn't be as well
Nor would the acts of any man
Be anything to tell

I think it's much more subtle than
Presented as Free Will or Not
The twin idea appeals to me
Identical or what?

8. Obscure Buddhist Poem

Blessed amongst all men
(And speaking as a woman)
What's it about then?
Being extra human ...

Filled with good things
In the way of being
This new life brings
An eclectic way of seeing

And why is that?
Have I done or been Other?
No, just a creature, me
One like Another

But it is quite right
All gold or glowing white
In amongst the soft air
That thing beyond compare

Inner ranges out wide
Within yourself but more beside
This day, this night
Strangely gathered, held tight

9. Yesterday I wrote a poem:

How good it is this precious time
Quite free from all the daytime tasks
A spacetime that pushed those away
And me, my mind, can wayward stray
The world retreated nothing asks

It's dark and quiet but for the clock
The early morning birds and I
One of the birds catching my mood
Expresses it within its cry
It's calling out an All is Well
Which bird it is I do not know
(It could be saying Bloody Hell)

The point is that I'm by my Self
With hours of freedom my behest
And birds rejoicing in the know
The person in this extra place
Is like a joy that's also rest
There's nothing gross and nothing base

I know I'm not the only one
To reach from mind up to this spot
Enjoying a serenity
Where black and white are simply not
And time is Now eternally
Resolved here are opposing facts
That separate our Yes and No
Our right and wrong and all of that

10. The God That Isn't There

So every hour enacts with love ...
The day has tasks and only asks to move
A modest skill or enterprise. The inner core
Elated, swells to so much more ...

It isn't God that God might be,
That rules myself and all of me
Devoted in its inner warmth
That gives the will, the aim the strength

So what is there that stills the noise,
The dream of God that with us toys?
It is most precious, is most good
How God would be if just God would

No Godlike figure with white beard
Nor sin accountant to be feared
But down with me and all unfurled
Within, without, through all our world

11. Change Poem

The beauty that is here to me
Will be quite changed with time
To different things, quite otherly
That might not with me rhyme

Revealed to be a private shape
With colour all unique
It's music I can hardly share
It's lines their own landscape

So beauty is a private thing
And relative to me, and sweet
Though Plato saw its aery form
That place where poets meet

Poems of Nature and of Place

12. At the Mayr

I want the days to cartwheel passed
Full of lovemaking and other plums
That delight me ...
Like sunlight on water.
There's an English lady
Stamps on walnuts,
Stamps on hornets too
And an Angel of the North
Like a boy, tall
But all woman
She bestrides mountains
While I get warm far below
On a bench in the sun
Thinking these thoughts
Green, lake lapping, thoughts
Not fast like moorhens
But dipping lazy
Like slow fishes wend
Or wishes gentle tend

13. Romney Marsh Murmur

Under the Saxon Shore hillside
Under a pale and wide sky
Grey in a soft and green languor
Out of sight of the home country lie
Lands all obscured and uncertain
Most of all to a bold worldly eye
Be ready for gentle renewal
Under the wide and pale sky
Listen and know the unseen there
Don't now make a query to why
Answer will come if you're quieter
Not if you strive hard or try
Into the deep Marsh meander
Lost in mysterious lanes
Water through rustle reeds watches
And conjures eclectical runes
Aery light colours are lucid
And gleaming in varying tones
The Marsh person cannot be spotted
Alone he will hear plaintive cries
Sheep are abiding their time here
In the land where eternity lies
Slowly beneath its brown tile lines
The church in a timeless way bows
Moisture seeps out of the acres
It moves in slow crisscrossing lines
To mirror this sight in the gloaming
A cream dinted comely moon shines
The Marsh person might be out roaming
With creatures a different life finds

14. Churches of the Heart on Romney Marsh

Like cottages and castles
But holy with more stones
Those quiet chambers of a quiet God
That merge the outer inwards

Create a gentle presence, feet in the grass
Deep as a person who knows how
Sheep talk to one another
And to eternity

We can own a God who lingers
In the willow trees, browsing a ditch,
Or lofted by a sunset of surpassing radiance
Floats in the moon of a dark sky

15. Marsh Poem, Morning

At five o'clock or near about
The sun was not yet up or out
The SOAY sheep were fast asleep
Dew, deep and lucid, on the lane
Above a long low line of mist
Those ruined towers rose up the sky
And far behind a row of ...
Towering treetops ... were aligned
Seeming a castellated plain
In Southern France or some such place
Not the quiet homely Marsh we know
But ground of Cathars and armed crowds
I paused before the awesome show
A day before were huge dark clouds
As background to a live rainbow
The others who are all in bed
Cannot imagine what I see ...
And every morning when I come
The chickens run to welcome me

16. Afternoon Walk, Canal Du Midi

On afternoons the time is long
The sunny hours flirtatious
They dance and bend in Einstein waves
They're gleefully curvaceous
And on and on winds the Canal

My mind becomes diaphanous
The stately trees hold onto form
The rest is coloured passionless

17. Afternoon Walk, Weary

I walk along for mile on mile
This walk is going to take a while
Then sitting down I cry a bit
And wonder: Will this make me fit?
I clocked ten thousand steps today
Along the brownish waterside
It's calming counting down the trees
As endless as the water is ...

18. Mirepoix Monday

We always go to Mirepoix, usually on Market Day
Parking is tricky and certainly a few streets away
Walking with anticipation towards the centre
We see houses striped with wooden beams
That are colourful and lean a bit from the true
Giving visitors a sense of great age
And of participating in a dance festival all at once
The lucky ones find the boulangerie and buy a jésuite
Before settling into the café, the one with the heads
Characters carved on the wooden purlin ends
Still here long after they inspired their friend
The wood worker, a carpenter, probably not dignified
With the title of a sculptor in those days
Going home to modest fare while
These centuries later we luxurious folk
Lounge in the café crowd and expect
To visit stalls heaped high with strangely expensive
Goods that one doesn't need
Last time I bought Nougat from Montélimar
At about a pound a bite but I was happy not like
The one who spent fifty euros on a piece of sausage by mistake
Inside the great church gloomy colours abound
Beneath high ceilings in huge arches round
There is a saint clenching his fist in a somewhat unsaintly way
And a font for Holy Water that ought to cure all ills
But has a plastic bottle of sanitizer placed on its rim
Indicating lack of faith in these unholy times
Filled with the fat, happy, jésuite eating ones
Of the late decadence of Europe

❋

19. London

London has a wedded grace
There's a certain place
Where I stand looking
For my lost love

I used to think of him
Thoughts drifting uphill to the Himalaya
But he's no longer there
Nowhere

Yet all around
And this the ground
Where I am with him
My heart lifts at Charing Cross
And more in bright weather
But also in the rain
Getting off the train
Bring here being near

Strangers that I see
Are kind to me sometimes
Sometimes I am kind to them
As well. And you can tell
There's good that's doing

I'm going on good
I'll give him a share
Redeem his sins burnish his soul
Make it whole
He wouldn't care
But he loved me so there

20. Moon

My friend the moon is always there
Safe part of enormous sky
Winking at times from pitch dark air
Softly to earth my watching eye

When large and round and golden red
I know that things will be all right
I think of the moon as I go to bed
It will be there on guard all night

Or pale and tender moon may seem
If we're up early and can see
She lingers like a thickened dream
And softly talks some more to me

The moon is distant if it's high
And far more formal when like that
At dawn and dusk she calls me nigh
The two of us will have a chat

A wordless talk of course we share
Of nothings her, of somethings me
Moon may have time can this compare
Brief intense me, continuous she

The other points we ponder are
The strange ways that we have of linking
Bringing us near or keeping us far
Feeling or Being more than Thinking

Poems Of Erotic Love

21. The Architecture of Love

I'd say he loved her a bit
Enough perhaps to fill an egg cup
But she could fill a house with her love

The house, surging with embrace,
Would swell its space
And hold a moment's trace
Growing in defiance
Into another, a mind world,
Not within the laws of science

He had a male conviction that he was
In some male way more of than her
She even half believed it
Though he was of no great achievement
His maleness was a sort of increment

I think it made the ceilings higher
And the walls bulge at times
Certainly he must have knocked his head
In the doorways

So he was comfortable
In ways that belied
His small love space
While she despite she tried
Had a house, created place
But remained homeless

22. Unrequited

Footprints on the earth, warm corn days
The air a haze. And me!
While he -
Sexless as a cloud
White, pale, quiet, grey
Drifts, does not stay
Thinking strained thoughts:
Not about me

And it hurts my eyes with tears
Stirs my fears
Of "No" unspoken but said
Where I so want to be instead

Alone and sometimes writing
Does he, my fragile heart
Squeeze constantly
Absorbed by words and thought
Doesn't he know? They ought
Alas, to be of me
Just one or two or three

His face is dark and he is hunched
Forward on the chair
I try not to stare
A blue dressing gown leaves his legs bare
Voice hard he questions me unfairly
Hours later sunny again
Aware of his sin he gives a grin
Sure perhaps
That he might always win

Hope today as he comes bounding in
Smiling boundlessly chin in the air
Hugging, punching, pushing me
And I enjoy the happiness
Even though he may not see
Any of it I do

And what then?
Is it a little bit of love?
Or just well-being, being boyish
Puppy-like, affectionate?
I love anyway
And must be wary
Be wary? Of joy?
Am I mad? Of course I am
Mad about a Mad Man

Would that I were
Happy as an angel dancing on a pin
Down here's quite dim with only him
And happiness is thin
At the sharp end of the pin

23. Minotaur

The man's a Minotaur
For all the glory of his looks
He is a monster

He has a labyrinthine heart
A place of many chambers
Wherein one hidden room
Does have a little love

His agony his roaring beastly self
Can't feel his way to that good place
The blinded groping is to get in
And that's the labyrinth

The puzzle's in his head
The search within
And he can't do it
Notwithstanding seeking thread
From lovely women

He just destroys them as he goes
He roars, he knows
He is a monster
He has grown horns and horrible

Inside he cries
His prison a heart maze
Where he can gaze
With darkened reddened eyes
But never find the way
Nor tell nor night nor day
Nor ever say this is the way

24. Power and Resolution

Raising an eyebrow slightly she asked
Are kneeling at my feet?
Watched as his body stiffened
In a pause

His eyelids raised a fraction
He murmured "Yes"
Then lowered again
To his task

Later his arm pulled her
Strongly towards him
Sliding her ribs,
Making her aware
Of her waist

"Look at me" he said
And frowned a little

25. Man in an Ice Cube (Myles)

It melts me completely when you're kind

But you're not that kind are you
I hoped you'd see
With open wide eyes
The size of my feelings inside
And beside
Why don't you know? Doesn't it show?

Once you gave a deep smile.
Then while I'm all soft
You'll be horrid

I'm never quite in time
To stop a sharp ice pain
Not a nice pain
Deft knives you hold
Blurred in all round cold

Man in an ice cube
Melt your way out in my direction

Forward projection
Can't wait for global warming
You'll be the last ice to go, I know

Meanwhile I drink
And there's the clink
Of the man in an ice cube
Imprisoned nude
Measure of all things
He can look and
With a glass eye magnify
My hand shook

Genius that's flawed
Diamonds in the air, sparkle in your hair
Yeah! Adored, you'll be a prize
Don't be surprised
It's a prize idiot, that has me floored
For when you smile I'm all Smyles.

26. The Kiss

I did think about that kiss
From time to time
The one you meant to give
That I asked for

And of your blue eyes
Head tilted to one side
Looking shy
So unlike the bold even forceful
Way you spoke in public

I thought that if you tried
I'd step aside
But then … I might approach
And touch, not much
A light almost kiss, a miss
A nearly there
In that space of air
That gentle urge
That hope to share

A pause, a poise, no noise
But still
The voluptuary thrill
It will be firm
Quite quickly
And withdraw
For more

Soon I lose the thread
Of what's being said …
Wordless my mind
Is otherwise rhymed

27. Girls and Boys

When I see a girl and I want her
It's so easy and I can charm her
And she's mine
I can tease her, boss her gently about
Be kind, toss her this way and that
Indulge her

With a man it's so different: if I like him
It goes without saying that he
Simply will not fancy me

Of course there are some who do like me
But I am offhand with them
Even cruel. And they suffer
(This gives me a mild pleasure)
But the ones I like are so difficult.

OK, so thirty per cent of me is fat
And therefore bound to wobble
But the other seventy per cent
Should be bone and muscle
Hard stuff. Not the kind of thing
That has the consistency of jelly
I don't understand it
How can things be so poorly arranged?

There were times in my youth
When I would move along
Followed by a wake of adoring males
Hopeful faces and forlorn or pleading eyes
Tossing on the crest of their desire
To have my attention
I liked this, well enough
But it didn't bring out the best in me

To get back to girls of course I love them
But they're so simple
Bit by bit they reveal
Their beauties and I enjoy these
But the point is, that I do not want
To do anything about it

28. Jamie

He felt quite different
Like a snake and a fury
Fierce, hot fast
Not forceful but deep
A fury but gentle

It doesn't make sense
When we met he was well pissed
We walked we talked
He kissed
Hurt he looked when I said No
He did not insist
How could I resist?

There wasn't much of him
Above the waist
But tired dark hair
Tired dark eyes
Those blinding teeth
And sweet soft lips

He was long, long legs,
Extending in a long, long penis
Like a Paris monument to look at
The eyes travelled upwards.

He was begun so well
But wayward, a musician
Painter and a drinker
Now where has his life gone?

29. He Stood There

He stood there, seeming alone in the room
A bar crowded enough but my mind
Was on him conscious as I moved about

And now I think, a sunflower
A palm, a stork, an elephant
He seems so glum and vulnerable
His hair and downcast head

Like a sunflower on an awkward stalk
Or a palm, tall, alone against the sky
And flopping a bit up high or about to
The stork its single leg top heavy solitary
And the elephant alone calm gray
Weighty solemn and wise

Why does he attend this place
Arousing tender concern
In the bosom of women round about?
But he's a man, heavy with thought, perhaps
All in the head anyway

30. A Poem for Jeremy

Jeremy's a shortish man
He's square and wide, from side to side
And going out with him is great
Because he tends to concentrate
On virtues that you scarce possess
But he will mention and profess
To be impressed with what he finds
Meanwhile bright gazing, so at times
You beam yourself right back at him
Happy without and happy within

Jeremy is handsome too
Just see his face from side to side
It looks with pleasure back at you
With even teeth sometimes on view

31. Foreplay

You shout into the phone
With magnificent dominance
And I am reduced to a laugh
You rightly recognise as hollow
You banned me from Email
Is the voice to be reduced
To a drop of tallow
Coagulated into silence?
Or dried, all angles like
The poor remains of a spider?
That voice that works in poetry
That wove words, that oiled
The wheels of meaning?
This is the binding of the feet
The bandage on the corpse
Even while still living
(And not even a Mummy)
We like gorilla power
We respond all right
But in the context of a *female*
And not as a *person*
In such circumstances
You, too, might have cold feet
If they were not made of clay.

Poems Comical and General

32. Upon returning to Consciousness

I drank the gas they made me take
I tried quite hard to stay awake
It wasn't like a normal sleep
But something absent, more than deep
I wish I didn't know that he
Has looked inside my right hand knee
Or rather that I too could share
The sight of flesh and bone in there
For he has done it once again
Sliced me open caused me pain
I'm reassured to know he can
The surgeon seems a cheerful man
Clean cut my leg and delve about
To get those bits of metal out
And when I woke the man's a whiz
He had completed done the biz
His eye is certain and he's deft
I doubt there's any ironwork left
And now for better or for worse
I've written him a little verse
And while yet still in dopey mood
I offer him my gratitude

33. Trouted

A lady walking to the lake
Fell in the water by mistake
And found she had become a trout
And found that she could not get out

The water sloughed her silver sides
Both cool and warm at once
She swam between the waders thighs
Proximity of pricks and cunts

Another clasped trout in their hands
Then threw trout on the bank
As trout reentered into man
The saviour fish to water sank

For love of them trout dived back in
Now round and round the lake they swim
For they are subject of a hex
And find themselves a single sex

Perhaps the Lord was furious
That people are bi curious
The Word of God should not be doubted
Against their will they have been trouted

34. Being Asleep

I am happy asleep
I don't know it at the time
But when I wake
I have enjoyed myself

Stretching so all the muscles seize
Legs swing around down
Feet on the ground
All day that way

But come the evening
Bedtime comes around
Soft the sound as I slip in
And move in hypnagogic
Worlds worth magic

35. The Politician and Chorus

The building's antithetical
To feelings rich poetical
And one must go outside to find
The deeper reaches of the mind
Oh! The poor man his life is hectic
Hope for him once but he has wrecked it
A glance to any side will show
The splendor that he'd better know

A politician ought to ask
Am I the man for this great task?
The modest Charlie Davies who
Manages our lifeboat crew
And helps the people as you ought to too
Six pounds an hour thanks that will do
Is a far better man than he
And ought to have an OBE

A Statesman can be very fine
Far sighted and with Good in mind
But how can that apply to one
Who travelled on the morning train
With thoughts assessing personal gain?
Oh that this too too solid flesh
The MP's covered in a layer of fat
Could rise again all new and fresh
It makes us feel quite strongly THAT
He hasn't suffered doesn't KNOW
The awkward things that touch us so
To dwell upon what's clearly good
And deeper values recognize
See kindness in a stranger's eyes

Back to the office, in higher mien
To look at the state's work again
He wonders:
Have I had a noble thought?
Do I know what honour means?
Are these the real things?
And not in-betweens?

36. The Grand

We're talking about THE GRAND
The one that's ... ... And
Up there on The Leas
Above the cliff up high
Huge against the clean wide sky
For all the world to see
It's monstrous large
Bentley in the garage
Kings and their paramours
Walked the sea shores
Strolled their ways
In halcyon erstwhile days
Now it's alive again
Tea in the Palm Court,
Known as the Monkey House,
Paintings everywhere
Writers here and there
In the old days
On the ballroom stage
She played a part, Sarah Bernhardt
And surely you saw Robert Morley
Or again Michael Caine?
Outside at a table listen
Jazz in Kepples bar smoke from your cigar
Moon shines a path
Smooths the waters of the sea
Meet me by the piano
On Friday meet with me ...

37. Holocaust Day

Holocaust Day and Leisers lost their lives
But many more and one this one survives
So I rejoice beneath the wide Marsh sky
Scarcely thinking how they came to die
An evil outcome of our science
The product line in bad appliance

The Bomb that brought war to an end
Was Man when men too clever tend
It was a triumph and disaster
The ones who thought it through soon after
Saw clear how we had gone too far
Do not rise up to follow any star

38. Brain Poem, Taormina, Science of Consciousness

And from the proud ingenious brain arose
À consciousness that knows itself it knows
It's hardly hard that being in the Now
Not only is the What but is the How

A scientist in the darkened musty hall
Waits, jigging slightly, his people to enthrall
The screen is lit, the mic is on its stand
His laptop and his acolytes at hand

And from the painful naked brain arose
À consciousness that knows itself it knows
It's hardly hard that being in the Now
Not only is the What but is the How

We're shown a map, some physics and some math
Those clever pictures surely are enough?
And back and forth we go about the brain
Philosophy, psychology in vain

And from the gentle patient brain arose
À consciousness that knows itself it knows
It's hardly hard that being in the Now
Not only is the What but is the How

39. Street Market Revel

If I say she's fat the sort of face you'd pull
But she's joyfully there moving along on her bicycle.
He certainly thinks so his arm protectively around her
Not that they move much being fixed at a crossroads
On the way into Revel somewhere in southwest France
We went there for the street market
Which is of great repute this I don't dispute
It is rather good no doubt and a jolly day out

40. Getting Older

I walk on upwards up the hill
The vineyards stand by brown and still
A sketchy crop fights with the mud
Courageous against deep winter's Will
The hedges are in timid bud
Along the rather battered track
I've walked a long way now I think
Perhaps I should be heading back
To eat some cake with a warm drink

I'm walking on a grassy knoll
The chateau was a worthwhile sight
And I keep moving on and on
My left-hand side and at a height
The white and shiny Pyrenees
Sky sharpened points designed to please
Look hard and pure as if to bite
Those bright keen angled Pyrenees
Would give a challenge to my knees

My knees aren't hurting me just yet
But warning me lest I forget
For I am aging just a bit
The length of human life is writ
In just two weeks my seventieth year
Whirls into time no longer here
It fades to something lacking trace
But for its pattern on my face

41. Morning Poem At All Saints

I am a happy lady
Walking on my land
My boots are good and solid
My tea is in my hand

I can see my donkey
She brays when she sees me
I can't give her a titbit
Because I'm drinking tea

It's early morning dawn time
Quite gorgeous in the sky
It's just like that inside me
My heart is rising high

I have to do the dung now
The geese are eating grain
The barrow's old and crumpled
There's been a bit of rain

I'm standing in the field and
The donkeys come across
Some birds are watching from the side
The sheep are in a posse

These are such precious mornings
Where would you want to be
Collecting dung effectively
Is good enough for me

42. At Oxford Station

The trouble with the young
is that they are young
Tumbling hair oversupplied
clumsy shoes

Blurred expression on faces
glossy but often spotted
Confused lurching movement
Many to many angled elbow limbs
Bumping bag dragging in masses
The odd one isolated
They go along

Not quite the sporting Gods of Olympia
Oh no,
Just the fatted calves of decadence
And no hope

No dress sense lacking grace of deportment
Having the discrimination of wild animals
Youth misses that beauty in an adult
That lies in moral discernment
Will take the lumpens years to acquire
By slow accretion
Even then
Missing many wholly.

But prejudice wait
Like Americans heartily disliked until a meeting
One to one
Is to be charmed impressed
To begin to think
The future in good hands
After all

43. Interfaith Poem

If interfaith you want to be
And really it's a must
Each school of thought must clearly
Be studied with a lot of trust

The Hindus know that God is all
The grounded range of Being
And if you answer to that call
You'll soon become All Seeing

The Muslims are a sterner lot
With manner that is formal
They hold the line for old time thought
Tradition being normal

A Christian goes with One in Three
Or is it Three in One
Their strength is welfare socially
And first class work they've done

The Jews are good and give a lot
They think they were the first
And from the Torah understood
Job keeps his faith
Through worse and worst

A Buddhist doesn't have a God
He works life from within
To calm detachment gives the nod
A state that's moral to live in

An atheist is reason tied
His world is black and white
A simple God he will deride
Constructive work for him is right

A manly Sikh, a gentle Jain
Confucius, Shinto, Tao
A brother Baha'i and then again
Let all religions take a bow.

For people all know bad from good
Those with a kindly heart
A friendly smile between us should
Blow all our differences apart

Allah and Yahweh, God or None
God the Father God the Son
A humane Spirit makes us One
When we're together we've *all* won

It is a state we can't ignore
We need it really more and more
So, can we hope that people may
Attain a valued Agape?

44. Thoughts Over Christmas

I am alone in a space
Created by winter
Keen to surrender
The Ordinary Thing
To move into that space
An unknown place

Into a wide world
Of self space
Unshared unprepared
At the strange pace
Of myself

I didn't volunteer
To be alone here
And I'm not fit or I don't fit
No family cheer
On the shelf

The snow the isolation
Gives to elation
At a complicit glance
Like the chance of sun
A shaft like laughter

Or smiles what fun
If I move out on a wing
And another thing
Others are also untouchable
Discretion in black holes
Between people

Also I am afraid of
Strange sounds
Only the pipes
Or snapping wood
But the danger
That a machine could ...

What? Fail in charge
Of this concealed life
My life my own
Of wanting to go on
In hard times alone

Hope over Christmas
Beset by poor odds
Others worse off
Poor sods
Silly fears, even tears
Foxes in the garden and
No one to talk to for DAYS

It's not a two way radio
In this house that says
Anything could happen
In space, in the snow
And who'd know?

✻

Poems for the Countries of the EU

45. Netherlands 1

The Dutch were double
Finger in the dyke
Finger in a Van Eyck
Would be trouble
Lots to like
Not Edam of course
And must force
the last of a rijsttafel
Feeling full
All those flowers
Reasonable folk
About whom one said
With respect the while
Notwithstanding the chuckle
Like a clog or liking
A blond head an open smile

46. Netherlands 2

Fifty years, two generations,
To speak of that dense
Cloud of time
I cannot see through the period
For its many misted happenings
But I'm here so too is Amsterdam

The heavy buildings decorative
Seemly and so strong
Are they tending to lean longing
Perhaps for a beloved
On the other side of
An unrelenting canal?

Bicycles lie angled in spider heaps
How dangerous on the road
The speed a moving of limbs
While trams are calm by contrast
And cars seem actually nervous
Unusual isn't it?

Good nature largely reigns
Museums do not disappoint
We have an acme of civilisation
And a cold debris of depravity
Clean healthy but contrasted
With the lifetime dream the things
That might have been

Those looking roundabout
Can everywhere be seen
The city is humane inviting
Each to that aspect of their state
That does predominate
Without judgement offering
Whatever is the song
You choose to sing

47. France 1

The rival country that
We love nearby
Exerts a fascination
We deny
The irksome flourishes
And pride we suppress
Admiration and ignore
Some of the glory
Or at least we try
But those dishes and the vine
Vain philosophy aside
Recognise that something's fine
Ought pinched lips chide
The other side?

48. France 2

Our nearest neighbour and our dearest foe
Between our countries travellers come and go
With smugglers refugees and more
The Channel is a crossing we adore
The French are good at roads and food
The pastries and the bread are fine
Street markets are quite glorious
We need not even mention wine
We British are a stalwart lot
Not ones to groom and preen
Our market towns and countryside
Are natural soft and green

Our leaders proffer the same rhyme
The bright but jowly version is
Our homely, unkempt sort of Prime
It's beer or ale it's not champagne
In Presidential sort of Fizz
Clever and slim and rather vain
The national pattern shows again

We like eccentric amateurs
Not national icons of past time
Matured at home in our own story
Not an attempt at courtly glory
Yet France has a fraternal code
With Liberté Égalité
The central thinking plays a part
While Britain wobbles on the road
Our classes and our wealth divide
Have proved so hard to set aside

49. France Another Day 1

Fine restaurants here are quite a few
A three-course lunch will surely do
And you must pay thirteen Euro
Once that is done well off you go
Of course you might try à la carte
And sample scrumptious lemon tart
My birthdays coming up quite soon
And on that very special day
I think I know what I would like
I think I'd like a cassoulet

50. France Another Day 2

Walking a little I can see
Wide stretches of the French country
The trees are cropped the hedges neat
An agricultural master feat
In England, Wales and Scotland too
We let the trees do what they do
They grow by nature wave their arms
And grace our more relaxed type farms
In France it's order all around
They have the landscape in control
Might we suggest on Freudian ground
That Britain has the female role?
Yet when it comes to actual war
The British win them rather more
We need not mention this today
As open war has gone away
And all of Europe is like one
Negotiation has begun
The rivalry is only local
On the world stage we are one people
The countries of the Continent
Are friendly now and of one bent

51. Germany

I was there in the city about the soft
Well managed countryside
For several days
Visited churches with great
But slightly comical stone sculptures

Saw too the rococo glories
The ones that cause
Slight nausea on recollection

Gladly mention the helpfulness
the smiles the relaxed strolling about
Fabulous cakes, daily coffee

Afghan staff duly German toe the line
At a meal on a high terrace
Overlooking vineyards
In Cyborg like compliance

It's good, it's proper
As must be you see
Comme il faut you know.

What upset me
Were the hard new buildings
Straight edged like a cut
Fronting each other with rigid faces
That abused and smacked
A delicate aesthetic sense
Not to say oneself
Showing no mercy

52. Sicily/Italy

It doesn't matter if it's shabby
When it's kind
Where higher up the hill there's art
To find
Not ART as forced might be
Rather a true built-in appeal
That all may see

The pottery, the plants, the image intimate
That touch us nearly too
As the good humour
And the loving laughter do
Humanity maybe it's not too late

I saw a tree so large it held a hand
To passersby who lingered paused to stand
And nearby was a garden grand
In layout in its age and really formal
But to locals welcome
And seem it must to them
Entirely normal

Glancing casual at the sea smooth blue
With Etna smoking in a distant view

53. Tory EU BREXIT Poem

When I think about a Tory
Do I feel a Righteous Fury
How could they win with Brexit lies
When I did not want to sever ties?

I love the whole great Continent
And hope the Tories will repent
Along with other hopeful men
I look to joining up again

The Labour Party was a mess
Which added weight to the distress
The Liberal Demos lost the chance
The best position to advance

Remainers did not mobilise
To make the voters realise
And worst of all the wretched Press
Gave Europeans Non not Yes

I shall think myself compatriot
Not care who likes it who does not
I'll love my neighbours and besides
This country where my heart resides

Pastiches on Great Poems of the Past

54. The Garden

(With Apologies to Andrew Marvell)

How foolish men themselves astound
By their own struggles in the round
Unceasing labour to attain
A prize that in the end is vain
Unseeing the abundant teem
Nor having more than he does dream
While all of nature to us shows
The simple path to what it knows

To rest while Men are toiling on
And never know when work is done
A deeper mind in innocence
Will flourish by the sweeter scents
Quiet plants are wholesome and they cure
The human turmoil that before
Seemed to me something to desire
While now it only seems bizarre

A colour of a soothing hue
Glows for me from the morning dew
No black or scarlet underwear
By harsh attractions me ensnare
A selfish lover's forceful glee
Cut crude initials in this tree
Attempting to commemorate
Glories that may be second rate

Partaking of a blissful ease
Amidst the fruits and flowers and leaves
Creative in a Lordly way
Like heav'n and earth in interplay
To dwell within a garden stays
The highest passing of our days
For Gods rejoice upon the earth
In sacred notion's fecund birth

What wondrous life is this we lead
To splice and mix a tiny seed
Abundant our inheritance
To make it better our pretense
The curious peach and nectarine
Combine and thus become obscene
Stumbling in science as we move
Ensnared in pride - do we do love?
Meanwhile within my heartfelt mind
That's deeper than the other kind
I softly whirl with happiness
Learning how gently to address
The worlds within the worlds that are
From me at this point very far
There's nothing I do care for less
Than pleasure in its noisiness

The iridescent water drops
Spray wildly on the nearby crops
Where those with subtle colours rove
In gold and grey, in rose and mauve
And I, or part of me, is there
To live more widely than I dare
My breath the wind and my delight
Refracted in the jewelled light

I, in my happy garden, can
Live quiet alone without a man
A choice of gentle paradise
That multiplies its glory twice
A taste of music of a mood
To honour deep sweet solitude
But humans do not have the part
To ply for all time at this art

Each creature follows its own rhyme
In God's created world of time
Ev'n blossoms show us how life goes
Between the Springtime and the Snows
Proud Man with his awakened stare
Is heedless of his proper share
To grab Life that's not yours to take
Might bring destruction in its wake

❋

55. Ozymandias

(With Apologies to Percy Bysshe Shelley)

I met a Doctor with a Crooked Wand
Who said: Two Nurses with a Van from town
Stand in the desert. Near them on the sand,
Half sunk, a shatter'd person lies, gone down,
With wrinkled lip with tears of cold distress
With neurons all vexatious in his head
Which yet survive, stamp'd on the life of him.
Some words that mock him, objects that led
To his condition beside him on the ground appear
My name is Mental Illness worst of things
Look on my state you others and despair
Nothing of hope remains: I am decay
A quite pathetic wreck, mortified, bare,
A lone and wretched man gone all away

56. The Sunne Rising

(With Apologies to John Donne)

Busy Creator, unruly Man,
Why dost thou thus,
Disturb established systems and cause fuss,
Must the whole world your sexual preference learn?

You do a service if you chide
Rough schoolboys and all others spite
You tell the world in art they need not hide
Of any love attaining height
Love, all alike, no season knows, nor clime,
Nor hours, days, months, which are the rags of time.

Delivering artist happy now are we,
In that the world's expanded thus;
Thy work gave ease of mind, and made to be
A warmer world, freely including us.
Shine here to all, and thou art everywhere;
All love thy offer is, and we within that sphere.

57. I Wandered Lonely As A Cloud

(With Apologies to William Wordsworth)

I wandered lonely as a cloud
That cold observer of the hills
When all at once I felt quite cowed
To see some dreadful daffodils
Beside the lake, beneath the trees,
Averse, I shrank, I felt diseased

Voracious, watching, all the time
And crowding me along the way,
The pollen spewing yellow line
Choked off the best part of my day:
Ten thousand felt I one by one,
Oppress me, leave me all undone.

The waves of horror rose; but they
Encouraged floral pageant glee:
Sadly I could not even say,
Leave me to my company:
I shut my eyes but little thought
To quell the mood to me now brought:

For oft, when on my couch I lie
In vacant or in pensive mood,
They flash back on that inward eye
Which is the curse of solitude;
And then my heart with fast beat cowers,
Threatened again by horrid flowers.

58. His Coy Mistress

(With Apologies To Andrew Marvell)

Had we but world enough and time
Your guilt, Young Paul, would be no crime
We would sit down and think which way
To clear your head and gently sway
Your thoughts to a much clearer path
Where mind is fresh and one might laugh.

I by the Ganges side have rubies found
You in old Folkestone still do sound
The miserable Old Testament,
Catholicised to some extent.

And you may, if you like, refuse
Conversion to my better views
To make my efforts subtle grow
Vaster than empires and more slow
(We do not want to tax your brain
And can repeat things once again)

An hundred years should go to praise
The mystic state at which I gaze
You'll get there in the end to rest
Your heartbeat quiet within your breast ...

Your gloomy tendencies will go
As Time like Light moves fast aglow
For none can live where daily norm
Is nothing but a thing forlorn
And guilt not Love holds dismal sway
And slows or fouls our daily play.

If not, we have a wretched fate,
Where Tennyson controls our state
Your proud red blood flows in reverse
Becomes instead a thing perverse
The tomb's a nice secluded spot
Where no one takes black pudding hot

Now, therefore, for it's always due
Become inside a richer hue
Arouse the heart again with hope
That's been oppressed and cannot cope

Ordain the mind to better things
That presently to worse ones clings
Allow a freedom and relief
From wrongly inculcated grief
The long persistent horrid Guilt
A Hell inside yourself has built

Poems For Particular People

59. English Lady

Soigné the evenings
Swirled in rich designs
With narrow slippers
Pretty

Large eyes, pink cheeks
And glowing confidence
Knowing confidence
Perched on a bar stool
Could be a bit of fluff
But is quite other stuff
Don't be a fool

Highly esteemed
Arched brows, white smile,
It only seemed,
She was a silly girl
A little while

Back braced she paced
Stepping with a jaunt
Unknown to her
To haunt
The dreams of children

She stamped on a walnut
Ate the soft inside
Fastidiously.
She stamped on a hornet
"It's happier dead"
She said.

No nonsense there
Children in her care
Take instruction shyly
She plays her part
Keeps up standards
From the heart

60. James' Birthday Poem

A large proportioned man called James
Entered our lives and changed our times
His big round tummy came in first
It was a wonder was his girth

But he was large in many ways
His heart was wondrous giving
He waved his wallet on most days
And aided others with their living

His brain prodigious fizzed and stung
And coming down the stairs he sung
Of GENIUS in all its senses
Noting with JAMES it all commences

It ends with James as well he thought
And other nearby people ought
To notice this. He surges forward
Breasting through life with all on board

Ebullient, large, life's other parts
Are quite neglected as he starts
His writing 'tis a big demand
The house's mundane tasks be damned

A woman, two or three or more
Should be nearby on hand for sure
For what about My Personal Life
He'd like to have a happy wife

So big is he, a manly man
He manages as best he can
His Will is mighty and his Charm
Allow him selfish without shame

Nor do we mind and with good reason
For he's a loving and enormous person
His sheer humanity is great
And all his faults does thus negate

61. Maygay

I wonder if I could write a poem
About my mother
In her quite recent time
In the years that were her prime
She was a rich girl and a beauty
But then I didn't know her well
As a mother she was mine
But never hugged
Or kissed me
I came to know her love
In later years
It soothed away the unshed tears
The confused sadness
Of adolescent madness

She had a lovely smile
Big mouth those generous lips
When she sang
As I remember in the nursery
The dog with love fixed eyes
Would rise and pad towards her
I needn't tell that she was loved
And the heart of things
In the family the power of ours
And hours and hours

I never thought she loved me
But I knew that she was there
She fed us with great care
She always thought of having fun
Days come days gone
Sunny days, skiing days
So were days done

Calmly in charge
And things went well
Cleaners cooks and gardeners
Did their jobs
Meals were on time
And plentiful
We were sturdy children

It just made such sense
The world a worthy place
All things in their place
With people in theirs too
If I no longer espouse her values
They are in me and now that she's left home
They arise unexpectedly

If I don't approve I love being her
In those moments. Being wrong is better
Being her than it could be being me
So I scold myself lightly
Secretly pleased to be her daughter
It brings on inner laughter
She wasn't perfect not at all
But she knew what's best
And there it was most often safe to rest
May be the same thing keeps me now

And how she did things in the garden
It all flourished
She was kind to certain sorts of weeds
And favoured the romantic
Balanced artistic flair
Quiet blooms here and there
The water spangled garden
Always drew one in

She took such care
With clothing too
Things handmade or from Harrods
Meant a lot to her
She went out to do her hair
Was she a vain woman

Perhaps but shy as well
And modest in her beauty
Although she knew they
Would do anything for her
She did not exploit men
But hid behind her husband

Now when I dream of Craythornes
Although she is not often there
Her presence halcyon
Is in the air
Just sometimes she sits
Dark in the corner
Being difficult as later on

62. For Sophia 60 On 27th January 2022

I met her one could say decades ago now
A brave young woman lovely to see
With gangs of children nearby on the grass
Outside that big manor house of hers
She had wide hats and heedless physical integrity
Giving confidence to her cheerful carefree moves
Drinking fine tea with hefty lemon chunks
After bathing she dresses each evening
And in elegance will then expound
On a point of intellectual curiosity
In some detail.
The next day on the building site
She might heave a sack of cement
Paint delicately round a window frame
Or as an accountant complete a tax return
She'll talk for long times solving a problem
With endless care and patience
For a friend
The young woman maintenant soixante
Grandmother to several already
Remains prima facie in my eyes
So talented she might have done anything
But has done everything instead

63. Seventieth Year Thoughts in France

I am going to be seventy and pass a line that's Biblical
All those joyful bulging years to vanish out of present time
And float away like soap bubbles round with iridescence
Holding the precious colours of my life
In a drifting line behind me
I know they will refine into air sometime
Even before they leave my longing sight
A residue the mere trace of memory
That's partly my imagination
I am on a bridge between worlds
The life behind that lingers in my mind
And what is ahead that looms
Like darkened hills verily a Cloud of Unknowing
Beyond which no one may go in body
Or in any shape that defines a personhood
Mind I'd quite like to be an iridescent bubble
And merging into air might be delicious
Maybe the signs are auspicious

I am in No Man's Land like Crusoe on an Isle
It is all mine I can be joyful here
As much as I like in between time and no time for years.
Years that do not have the markers of a span
That defined period that stage is gone: and I am magical
Feet may not even touch the ground

Can I fly? What will I do? Does doing remain even valid?
Have I entered instead further into Being?
There's a divide between appearance
And the inside where one may dance with flowers
Tinkle with bells rejoicing in a quiet inward way
That might glow and light the face
To a quotidian world which let's face it
I still inhabit in some way and look
Rather solid no matter what is real

64. So Rupert ...

So Rupert have you really gone away
Your death leaves our reality in play
The mind is fractured into parts
A truer Rupert shapes instead our hearts
That cold-faced, purple-clad and bony corpse
A shirking mind will not admit to thoughts

High stepping at a quite outrageous pace
He moves around the town from place to place
A kindly eager forward-moving man
He wants to tell you everything he can
His record humming with attractive acts
Describes him as an architect of facts

We said he was a person without sin
Who knew about the pain that he was in
He walked by that Canal too near an edge
Then jumped or tumbled through the standing sedge
Ice cold the water, calm, though he be wild
It was a place that loved him as a child

A good man left us on that freezing day
Cruel days continued on their busy way
Release from time for him left us a gap
A warp for which we didn't have a map
As obligations to a death unfurled
It closed without him to a lesser world

65. Senegal Poem April 2022

Five white haired travellers meet again at last
Decades ago they shared the same time-space
Naive, in youth and beauty only, strong
Now come together to review the past.
A sixth is lost, perhaps this song for her
She was so modest, surely she'd demur
I'll list the others now that I've begun
A brief description each and everyone
Land Rover man who loved a big machine
He farms now on the Norfolk coast
Musician, sculptor and a beauty queen
The third a tender hippie cared the most
The next a scientist of fish and birds
Later a lot of admiration won
By taking trekkers to the Amazon
The fifth a poet with a way with words
She was a posh girl wouldn't do her share
She didn't notice or she didn't care
And one an optimist of quite eternal youth
Who studied stars while standing on the roof

Sahara down to Senegal it's miles
Did we set out and hope to right a wrong
To find it good or make a better place
In many photos we are wreathed in smiles
As baby boomers in an open world
We looked as if we were the gilded young.
Our minds were generous and our eyes were wide
That purity, through dire adventures, for us spoke
Dead camels, dust, armed men, mechanics failed
And some men's lust and goods were lost in sand
Our budget really something of a joke
At times those open eyes were eyes that cried

Their beauty surpassed ours in the new land
Agrarian but fit and full of hope
We did suspect no harm and none was found
We took in much our minds became profound
In lives thereafter all of us expressed
The lessons learned, no cynicism grew
We each got older, yet, in all of us we knew
To trust, to love, to openly explore
And that in giving we are given more

These five now, three score years and ten
Are back together all of them again
The world in part is better but in much it's worse
We have as others do a tale to tell
Of how we tried in life to make things well
Our gift to widen contact learn to share
With men and women everywhere
What more adventures will we have in years
Now made more precious by their being rare
To offer something and perhaps enhance
The lives that all along have been our peers
Be rather thankful to have had the chance
To steer the world a bit in its advance

66. Not Richard Dawkins

We float on the joy of unreason
Those of us who are not Richard Dawkins
I say at once his work is good
Quite good in the sense of very Richard
Not intending to shave it down
The God Delusion is funny too
And altogether correct
Within the limited range of the intention
Science *is* as wonderful as R D says
But poetry and filled heart's desire
Don't flood his neurons
In staccato bursts
Or any other overwhelming way
Unkindly left on a dry edge
Where reason is a structure
Building a hard shelter on a desert island
Telling the truth and good and earnest
More than a national treasure
Not made of gold, not a precious stone
Nor carved exquisitely. To be literal, Richard
We would let him into heaven
Perhaps more because he loved his wife so much
Than for other things

Poems of the Last Century, Younger Woman

Introduction

These poems were all written while I was living in India. During the hot summers we were generally resident at Scottsburn Estate an old colonial bungalow that we had restored in the Landour Cantonment area of the Mussoorie Hill Station in the Himalayas north of Dehra Doon. The mountains were high and steep – all very shocking to someone brought up on Romney Marsh, a calm flat land, lying in part below sea level on the south coast of England.

In the winter, when not on one of our magnificent tours about the various large states of the subcontinent accompanied by a dog, a cat and a tent, we stayed on land we owned on the outskirts of the capital near Najafgarh. We had eight acres in the village of Samaspur Khalsa, the grandly named Maya Danav Estate, where I was happily engaged in building a philosophical and artistic palace.

These contrasting landscapes make their appearance in many of the poems. As with other references they may seem unfamiliar to a European reader. I have divided the early poems into four groups. However they are almost all about the deep emotion in which I was afloat.

The emotion was love at a high and all enveloping level. Love of God, love of man, love of life and of nature. These loves may seem confusing to the reader but in each image or metaphor it is clear to me, at least, which love is involved. The confusion might arise from an unfamiliarity with the Hindu understanding that God is the ground of reality and being in touch with that ground within ourselves, is the purpose and fulfillment of life.

Access to this ultimate state is wide ranging but includes direct apprehension, the path of knowledge, that of meditation, erotic love, aesthetic engagement, dedicated work in the community, devotion and by way of nature. In the poems I am generally attempting to describe the impact of the experience on me in the multiple ways of everyday life. As the experience itself is indescribable I am bound to have failed but perhaps the words offer a glimpses ...

Briony Kapoor November 2024

Human Love or Love of Man

1. You Bid Me

You bid me meet you on a lonely shore
And there I waited for some hours or more
It seemed you were in everything around
Within the sky, the sea, about the ground

A black bird landed at my feet
And it was you, I heard it speak
Then slowly grew the figure of a man
And touched my lips and touched my hand
Then all of me became the sea
In endless meeting with the land

2. Musing

Oh, darling, why don't you come home?
My heart is troubled sitting here alone
Fear spreads desolation: I am hardly strong
To last your absence for so long

I wash my clothes
And hang them in the fragrant sun
I am waiting for my lover
I press them fresh, dry, one by one
I do wait for you forever
Will you hold my hand dear man
Suspended delicate in love I am
Comfort me as you only can
I want no other

Whatever we could do is done
Know I not that: ten years are passed
What is in life has come
I feel such reverence now, my dear
Emotion rousing up too much inside
Flows over from my seeing eyes
And you, you ask – why these tears?
Then we laugh: love hums in many airs

Oh tease me, darling, My heart laughs from it
This is your love, my life swings on it
I'll stay with you where love is in the air
Indeed for you my love is everywhere

Though when, by chance,
Some horrid demons steal
Upon my love from deep
His heart within
I cannot then, no chance,
That deep enchantment feel
That otherwise illuminates
The time I spend with him

But the commitment:
Warm weight of an arm
Over my body at night
Risking life for my honour
While wrong imagining that
I give his to the bazaar
Is this not love?

So I sit, that one away,
Knowing my womanliness
In solitude: black and white
On either side of dusk
We are loving through the grey
Inseparable continuous
As night and day

3. Desire

Oh Lord desire
Anticipation
I faint for the hour
And exaltation

Now this is him
Sensations crowd fall dim
All yearning me
Thither directed be

Hotly aroused
Towards you flew
My limbs trembling
Orderless withdrew

Kissing my thigh
The heat of our desire
Has burned your lips
And I am branded there

Before you bow
What am I now?
Ah, only this
Ever mounting bliss

❁

4. Hang Over My Imagination

Since meeting you my imagination
Has leapt boldly forward into heaven
Withdrawing now from that embrace undoes me
What joy your love has brought me darling mine
Exalted was my pleasure, now my pain
In the dark side of the situation tortures me.
And when you did not come
My heart died a little bit, little bit

May my body wither its round beauty
My love wasted like a flower unseen
If you cannot have them, why should they stay?
With what relish I felt my power against
Your desire – did you stop loving me
Or has love fled from neglect, from busyness
From the conventions which prevented it?
Courage is not alone sufficient when the
Dimensions of the world do not let us in
And we cannot increase them with love's power

Your image comes unbidden to my thoughts
To revel there with me: as thus you looked and
Thus you spoke that touched me so with pleasure
Still your smile stays about me your words your
Ways hang over my imagination
Those days of love so godly they clotted
Eternity in time, erasing the
Passing of the hours, so then and now
Always present, always present perfect
The desire which devours me, feeds me too
We are close to destruction when we know
Fulfillment in its grand intensity

5. Magnificently Male

You, magnificently male
Arrested all the world awhile
To your man's will took me away
Holding all time, all space, at bay
A ground abundant with emergent things
I laughed received your rain and grasped
The great male strength you entered in

In my sex weakness I desired
To give you all the burden of my life
And manliness I bowed to thee
I offered all my love
You took the same and honoured it
So thus I came to benefit
Though to my woman, man you be
Now do I value other pure integrity
Who want to be beyond my sexuality
Fear that great dark lord loom beyond me

6. Latent Pure Love

I looked at you with eyes of love
You proudly kept yourself away
It scorched my soul to come you near
All trampled tender feelings lay

In love I did approach your door
My heartbeat come my mind
My eyes were tight with tears unshed
A joyful fear filled all my head
Desire entire my frame did smart
All rational caution left behind
In overpouring by my heart
That little thing that was my mind

Hot love to ashes instant turned
By your cold heart
All molten passion petrified
On contact with that cruel willed part

Desolate all of me was gone
To loving you but I had none
Dark and empty I gave yet more
The right to even feel desire
Latent, pure love, exhaled was
In that hard condensation
More valuable than you alone
This hard earned compensation

7. Biting My Lips

Biting my lips and tongue
Still I cannot prevent
Tears in my eyes
Lower my head, turn away
Yet they sting bitterly
Threaten to overflow
The preventive lid
Revealing my state
To whom may see
So boldly lift my chin
Turning my face
To the clear air
Open eyes begging
Fresh wind to dry them
And restore my pride

8. Darling, I cannot ...

Darling, I cannot meet your eyes
I love your modest, moral
And your steadfast ways
My eyes would, guileless,
Tell you everything
Desire for me would
Revolution
To your manner bring
Sweetly contained, thus,
Near your person, I
Softly radiant, inward know
Which could not from
Lovemaking eyes
Towards you, outward, flow

9. Passion Worn

Your black eyes looked a challenge as I left
Or defiant, or pleading, I cannot say
I only glanced and did not linger
Eyes on eyes to understand
Holding together at that leave taking
For but I laughed, I talked
Your words were black splinters in my heart
Rejection spoke, all me was bitter stung
Darling, you did in this thing do me wrong
Who trembling a passion torn
Wrought pathway to your door
I, love, all love, my love placed you before
And fool I am thus knowing tears of pain
Do never mind but long for you again
In your arms now you see me cry
Oh, I have waited for so long
You know my wooing has your doorstep worn
Dauntless my bright pride but you neglected me
Furious, humbled by desire, I came
Still you rejected me
There is no wonder that now with you I weep
Like your threshold I am, inside, worn deep

10. Dahlia

My husband picked a dahlia
And brought it in to me
He placed it in my hand and said
I've brought this in for thee
And I was filled with love for him
Then feeling love-like-power
My heart, my mind, the rest of me
Became just like that flower

11. Love and Fornication

We are making love all the time
Man and I
What exactly is the significance
Of a fornication?
A woman may have it
Merely by lifting her eyes in the street
For a man – well – he suffers from lust
Poor thing
He lets us know all his distressing
Oh, let him have it
Poor thing

12. Servitor

Wrapped in a shawl
Servitor came
And tended me
Quiet fiercely

His master's lady
Dark, tall, surrounded
Must not be harmed
He is commanded

Every near move
He is aware
Noone may come
Nor none stare

Protected, treasured
Possessed I am
I know your love
Through serving man

13. The Alchemist's Dream

There was the alchemist's dream at dawn
In gold and silver and lead
The alchemist tall had told it all
The vision at dawn confirmed what he said

I was a humble helper of his
I waited by the fire
Patient for triumph, travailed in awe
Then beauty of molten gold I saw

See you wizard, alchemist, dear
In faith and love of you
I've taken what you scarcely hoped
As precious metal to prove it true

14. Be Near, My Love

Be near my love and touch your lips to mine
Remember love is outside space and time
Mark in the earth your footprint by my own
Eternal 'tis as Buddha's traced in stone
What meaning that our eyes meet in the glass?
Still stand beside me, my beloved friend,
This mystery is communion beyond hours
That eye to eye by heart and heart doth send
The touch that smooths so lightly there your skin
Distant from me is felt myself within
Press mine a moment with your passing hand
Profound the comfort that I understand
The slow enhancement love has undergone
Ensured to us that space and time are none

Divine Love or Love of God

15. Strange Intimate Union

Earth is body of the disembodied pure
Here we are grounded our ideals are sure
Rendered of deep dark seeming is more rare
But by a passion all of us are found
To be of earth and yet ourselves earthbound
Nor alone the earth, nor by itself the air
As in their union strange intimate the pure

Who taught me that desire is cosmic
To my such yearning I should yield myself
Throw round my arms grand to embrace this earth
With grave exultance in the beauty absolute
Of dark love bound to sing about its form
Time swelled heart in ages contemplate
Being more mighty than a thousand worlds
While sweated brow with diamond drops and pearls
Scatter about enormous strides to take
And learn at last slow beauty of the work?

16. Tossing The World

I am in love
With all the world
And all the world
With me
I toss world
In my hand
World tosses me
Don't speak of man or history
Cosmic aeons pass
Maybe
My love, the world
And I
In mutual glee
Playing with love
I pass this earth
With thee
Playing with earth
Earth jealous lord
Binds, bruises me
Playing his game
Or rough, or tenderly
Playing with love

17. Love Strewn

Lulled in the ocean lap of God
I hold life vibrant in my hands
Wholly my heart beats through the world
Earth licks my limbs
Wind calls my longing
Over vast lands
Throughout the puissant air
To twirl the sunlit leaves
Caress fulfillment in a flower

Hell and heaven are overthrown
About them both my love is strewn
Grass tickles tender like desire
Flowers, stars, raindrops,
Dance the air
Passion diffuse clouds overblown
Within it all my pleasure moan

18. By the Mahanadi

By the Mahanadi
I sit quiet all night
Stars finger me
With delicate starlight
Warm air round me wraps delight
Nature revealed is subtle bright
I am not here
Though seem I might
Essentially
I am the night

Or am I a star
Star deep of sky?
The rest is nothing
Elated am I
Oh! I am glad
Glad at once to know
The exalted above
While yet embraced below

Now stop my heart
Or slow your beat
So that I may
The whole world greet
Giving to world
I do find there
Myself transcended
Everywhere

❋

19. Love Life

The long shadow of love
Reaches all sides to embrace
On whom it may fall
Encompassing any
But joining only those
Who notice it
I was only young and new
When to its orbit touched
And fused, then drew
Towards the centre over years
Where after struggle, tears
I spiraled into ecstasy
And there eternal grew
Together hour and aeon
Bright I see
Whole life is just apprentice
To a future that will be
Gloriously stretching time
Stretching in beauty
Interior, my love,
You are to me
That swelling up
There's nothing left
Exterior to thee

20. Laughter Deep Inside

A surge of laughter deep inside
Absorbs the lesser I
My bones are teased, they tickle me
My heart without myself doth fly
And all the rest moves skippingly
Oh, happy mood do not subside
I find me on a dizzy path
That leads about a cheerful world
I drink a dazzling diamond draught
How merry I am here unfurled
To pleasant in myself reside

21. Mosquito

Mosquito tumbling
Sideways through the air
Tickling my arm and
Tangling in my hair
I hear your singing hum
And know you're there
Why should I dread your
Presence and your sting
If we are both
Created from one thing?
If feasting on my blood
Your satisfaction is
Then drink your fill while
I lie here in peace
My God expanded heart
My fretted nerves will ease
And you, my little darling,
May do just as you please

22. Diamond Life

Life is diamond
Inside mystic light
Soft coloured, gentle
Outside hard and bright

Dazzled and reflected
World does not know this
Within the carat cut aspects
Existing jewelled bliss

23. I Have Poured Myself

I have poured myself out into the world
For my heart was calling to the universe
I do direct myself now to the edge
Beyond which great energy rolls unknown
Ache in searching, sweetness in discovery
Enter the realm of God having freedom
In hard controlling thus the heart and mind
To feel, to know, to make reality
Thus can I do who am myself the world
One all significance, in all is none
Changing in time's endless manifest

24. Windbourne

I am no longer windbourne
Bones hit hard upon the ground
For beside the muddy water
Heaped is yellow flesh of men
Who have lived and suffered pain and died
Who will now do so again
As I walk I know that men may die
For they cannot understand
What's there between the earth and sky
Revealed in the opening of the mind

But see the birds upon the brick kiln
Plump and grey in red brick dust
Here and there amongst them
Subtle secret flash of rust
An old man with a buffalo
Greets me with hand to head
And I bow to him as brother
Though I know we'll soon be dead
We are three who know, before we die,
Opened to understand
What there is between the earth and sky
Revealed to our kindred mind

25. My Life Is A Secret

My life is a secret within me
That grows and exists by itself
When I'm happy or joyful it fills me
Then I'm one with the world and complete
If I'm sad or confused
When I'm lonely or low
Embrace me with comfort and still me
My spirit, my pure truth
Flower my love and grow
Fill all the universe for me
My edge will fade away to nothing
My sensations be confirmed in ecstasy

26. Live With Life

To live with life and happy be
A heart athwart with flame
And know the great unfolding
Of this scarce imagined game

Fulfil it if desire arise
Take it no more than swatting flies
Desire unsatisfied will sour
Your simple being in the hour

Life is only this or that
Of boundless joy a part
To understand it wonderful
Need be our only art

27. Sin In A Mad Mind

There is no such thing
As dirt or sin
See how I rub myself
In the soil
Over and over
Staying clean even
Glowing with renewal
From fresh contact
With other and myself

There is no germ
Or thought of filth
Only the mad mind
Of the fallen man
Says so
Through which we pass
To our best moments
Well, knowing this
Can we not let love
Dissolve the wall
Completely away?

28. World Without Time

Is the whole world here created
That I may laugh with joy?
Laugh who may be elated
Who too may world with toy
Time stains not here as we are told
Weave our passing through its layers
Illusion that we may grow old
All may herein be players
Thoughts embroidered threaded gold
Design is there, emotion bold
World and time before it bow
That which is real may only grow

29. Dark Sweet One

A perfect example of love I saw
One day when I went out
I yearned to know its nature
All about
So went and looked
And longed and looked
I went and stayed nearby
Until I knew it well, my heart
I could not keep away

I walk round and round where love is
Harboured in my heart
To proudly wondrous
Gaze on, pause in
Dark, sweet one, you
I dare not too directly come
What if love disappear?
Before you who are fine
My coarseness mayn't appear

I'll live on air
A thousand, thousand years
So long you're there
Dark, sweet one, you

30. A Bending Tree

I saw beneath a bending tree
That time was waiting there for me
Netted about in golden air
While all the world was within there
Now where am I who am outside
Time's form elliptical?
Am I eternity inside?
I laugh but I cannot tell
How often we are tantalised
To glimpse perfection clear
And dull those souls thus magnetised
To find they're only here

Contents of the Second Volume Section Three

Nature

31. Who Live Upon A Mountain

Are we in the world
Who live upon a mountain?
So many layers in the sky
And levels solid passing up to grey
Am I the bright light pouring in through there
Or am I moistured green
Like leaves dissolved in air?
How may a valiant daisy
Dare to face this life
Throw challenge to an oak tree
I, too, am here on earth?

Some of the rain that's falling
Lies here upon the lawn
While some deep to the valley
Will down and down be drawn
That which above, my soul,
The sunlight clearly lit
Below do mingle, ah me,
In the mud and grit

32. Feathered Identity

I once became
The feather of a bird
And knew a whole existence
In that horny shaft
One end I merged
Within the bird
And feather tipped there
Dissolved in air
It was enough
How I laughed

33. The Atmosphere Is Honey

The atmosphere is honey
A rural tranquil place
And flowers are orange sundrops
Grass, soft and dull ...
He ploughs the land like a lover
How he my heart doth lull
Earth turns deep, fresh
Falls back there to caress
Rich the soil and so proud
Like a lover to be ploughed
Pale quiet green
Do sooth and satisfy
Deep within the eucalyptus trees
Blue sunlight sky may only tease
The fringe of me, who muted pass
In cool, on grass
Beneath the eucalyptus trees
Green place this earth do comfort me
In it I move or quiet still lie
And here shall also maybe die

34. Spring Garden

I went into the garden
The plants burst into flower
Was it that my mood of love
Commanded nature's power?
Iris, daisy, clover,
A tender green leafed tree
Sprang outward to their friend the sun
And laughed and smiled at me

I also saw a butterfly
Perhaps the first this year
It lurched about with wide, white wings
Upon resistant air
I dabbled in my happy heart
And knew my love was there

35. Sun And Moon

There goes the sun
In the morning clouds
As dim and small
As the moon
And twelve hours later
Above the hills
Comes the moon
In the just same place
And I see them as I lie
Twice in a day
I am blessed by them
At seven o'clock
And at seven pm.

36. Storm

The clouds are yellow bruises
Bright white hail stings on the glass
The wind has pushed my eyelids back
Leaves blow in upon the grass

It's light beyond the mountains
With the early signs of dawn
Strong green trees are trembling, laughing
As I am upon the lawn

Pink tears the yellow atmosphere
Lightening at heart of me
The world indeed is awesome
But of beauty not of fear

37. Rain Diamond

I saw a diamond in the tree
The tree was dark, dark green
Blue, red and white
With diamond light
It shone there in-between
And tentative was passed to me
Direct to my heart but tenderly
A light and lovely jewelled strain
Arising from the moment's rain

38. Breeze

A breeze passed through
The sunny rain
And tossed the golden flowers
The brightened grass
Danced back its heart
One of nature's present hours

So I passed through
The sunny rain
A black sheep followed me
Its wool ruffed crystal
Danced my heart
Thought I
Where may tomorrow be?

39. Mist

Mist is soft and tears gently
Parting company with itself
Floats here and there
Between the mountains
Over the trees

I had a mouthful of mist today
And wrapped my tongue around it
It prickled my cheeks inside
Tenderly provoking me with
Hints of food and graver
Hints of suffocation

Other Poems

40. Delight On Guard

I drag about my hopeless days
My face is blank and pale
Delight seeped off in devious ways
Voice throat my barren wail

Nothing ignites my mind
My flesh is mud
Life empty is but rind
Dull, dull my blood

Deadened my earth is hard
That loved me often sweet
Why are you on your guard?
Delight for you I wait

41. Friend

Why did your heart fail, dear one,
Was it bad then?

I would like to press in th' earth
Where you lie

Cold and lonely place, but peaceful
Are you become earth then, dear one?

Wind sounds in the trees, tis you?
I am waiting

I look sad around, nowhere,
Art, dear one?

42. The Cock

A cock climbed on a heap of dung
And built his place there proud
He glanced about with bright bold eyes
He crowed and crowed aloud

To other cocks he showed his spurs
He threatened them with power
They left him room with his strong beak
His own great glory to devour

He saw his work, he heard his call
Imagined flocks of hen
He thought they would admire him all
And built and crowed again

He crowed upon the heap of dung
Desire was running riot
How he would hold them to the ground
And love them in the dirt

For years and years he carried on
Absorbed in his own great din
While world and life passed swiftly by
And disregarded him

The hens were laying eggs all round
Of others not so proud
Our cock discounted this because
He felt above the crowd

Now it so happened that one day
A round and rosy bird
A stranger, passing by that way
The mighty crowing heard

She turned her pretty head and saw
Our hero on the dung
And dazed with love she waited there
Completely taken in

The cock upon his strutting path
From time to time glanced round
And so he noticed her at last
Submissive, waiting, on the ground

He cocked his comb, he scrambled down
And took up a new stance
His heart was beating fast with joy
He thought: Here is my chance

He looked at her, grew mad with lust
A plump and lovely bird
To his dismay though knew he must
He could not say a word

She waited quiet for some long while
Then shyly turned her head
And flashing up her eyes at him
I love you Lord: she said

He made a move towards her
But he found that he was scared
He hoped that he might mount her
But he was a stiff old bird

She rubbed her glossy feathers
Against his trembling chest
She waited for him patiently
Encouragingly pressed

All the great visions of his life
Were focused on her now
But when it came to action
Well, he just did not know how

A tear was sparkling in her eye
Oh, please don't go: he said
She turned and threw contemptuous
Some dung upon his head

43. Lament to Time

Oh, wait a minute time
I haven't had enough
If you go on so fast
I'll soon be finished off
What is the meagre tally
I can put before you here?
Only twenty or so lovers
And some thousand pounds a year
My house, of course, superior to Jones
Three children who don't care for my old bones
Together with some honours which
However give me little cheer
I see through it all more clearly
With every passing year
We know we live to know we die
Avoiding this we learn to lie
And social status wear with pride
Ourselves and others taken ride
Already wrinkles cover brow
I do request you, Time, pause now
Reveal me something of the art
Of the eternal in our passing days
Time slowed not but it did impart:
Within me only the Eternal lies

44. London Bus Horror

I once got on a London Bus
And to my horror saw
A row of women all alike
With grim and heavy jaw
With curls of iron and leaden eyes
Their handbags clasped on thick spread thighs
They, dreadful, did not hesitate
With merest glance, or slight grimace
Acting together, robot eight
Gentler spirits to outface
Instead of human their demeanour
Was something like a suit of armour
Sisters, you are part of us
How have you come denatured thus?

45. Alienation

In those days mind was not filled
With thoughts like these
And man went about simple tasks simply
Now he cannot leave himself alone
To wonder deep in ordinary things
But is living in a dream like madness
Where reality comes with the shock
Of horror, and achievement
Is competence in every day work
We cannot disorient the mind
And lightly get away
Believing only reason is of common sense
While passion is the God insane perspective
Instead we find that man is mad
Slightly mad from isolation
He cannot do his simple work
Without resentment
Needs must force himself to act steadily
And knows not how to love

46. In The Bazaar

You call me Champa
Thin boy on a cycle
You laugh and I laugh too
For we are glad with knowing beauty
Rickshaw man and me
Then a smile
At the moving aside
Of a yellow monk
And glimpse of heels ...
Tall girl with the long plait
You've grown out of your clothes
It seems!
See love passing
In the bazaar
On an ordinary day

47. Plaint

Take delight from the air
See delight with the eyes
And my heart laughs in me
While people smile to see
How touching the earth
Doth comfort me

Black heart, oh, Man
That thus can thrust
Iron fetters on the world
Wherein I play
Till you hard hurt
What was so gay

I did not want but that
Trembling tender fingers
World might
Touch me through
Ears, eyes, all
Shivering beauty
To airy enthrall

48. The Dragon

A dragon dreadful came for me
Who young were dreaming here
Upon green grass in mist I lay
And sleeping soft I could not flee

That dragon gorgeous closed with me
Over my naked back to lour
Arcing its red, gold, huge scaled neck
To show its dragon power

I lay quite still in love and fear
It opened darkly gleaming jaw
Saliva dripped upon my back
A dragon odour sweet and raw

Who were you dragon to evoke
My love and fear so deep?
I never forgot you when I woke
And half I long for you in sleep

49. India Laughs Ceaselessly

India laughs ceaselessly
Who knows the merely temporal
And how we feel as
Our passions come and go
Oh, cruelty!

But is there something comforting
After all
In the gentle chuckle of eternity?

50. Wink In Eternity

When before was quite unconscious
And after may be too
Life is an unexpected turn
In eternity Which has a depth of meaning
We know at once
And recognise should not be wasted
Like the wink of a formal man

About the Author

By way of biographical information I am the second child and second daughter of a country GP who fled Germany in the 1930s. He married my mother who was beautiful, wealthy and fun. As well as my sister, I have two younger brothers. We had a comfortable upbringing - if going to public school can ever be called comfortable - but a happy uncomplicated home life with ponies, dogs, games of Monopoly and happy skiing holidays.

From a Conservative background I became an open minded liberal and floating voter after the great discovery of idealism in my early twenties. Lucky to be a Baby Boomer by generation, I am an emotionally stable extrovert by personality.

During university at Newcastle upon Tyne where I studied sciences and Psychology, I was able to travel widely and undertake adventures including a long distance horse ride and a trek over the Sahara Desert and down into Senegal.

After graduation I lived for a few months in Paris in the traditional romantic location of a garret near the centre. I returned to London uncertain of my path but there, quite soon, I met and married my husband helping him to run an art gallery for the ethnic arts in the Covent Garden area of town near the Seven Dials.

The two of us, he was a brilliant academic of Indian origin, lived in India from 1980 to 1996 when I returned to Europe to build a life of my own initially from financial need and then following the sudden death of my husband after a marriage of twenty five years. For many years now I have run a modest art foundation on Romney Marsh in his memory. There are of course many stories of these times but one thing at a time and this is the time for poetry.

By further chance and as a result of the historical facts of colonialism and the two great wars of the 20th century I, an ordinary Englishwoman, believe that I am entitled to seven different nationalities. I am also variously engaged with a number of different religions because of my personal history.

Briony Kapoor November 2024